W9-DJC-109

To Carol,

Thanks for bringing
+ welcoming me to RUC
Poetry group. It promote
Fellowship + Friendship Through
Poetry

Love
Peter VD
3/7/07

MEDUSA'S OVERBITE

A Book of Poetry
By
Peter V. Dugan

WYSTERIA

Long Island, New York
www.wysteria.com

Published by Wysteria
First Edition 2000
First Printing

Printed and bound by Acme Bookbinding
Charlestown, Massachusetts

Library of Congress Cataloging-in-Publication Data

Dugan, Peter V.
    Medusa's Overbite / by Peter V. Dugan.
        p. cm.
    ISBN 0-9651162-4-7
        I. Title.

PS3554.U366 M4 2000
811'.6--dc21

00-043417

ISBN 0-9651162-4-7

Contents

MEDUSA'S OVERBITE

Inside the Shadow

Outside the Garden

Facing the Wall

Danger: Deep Water

Do not go beyond this point!
There is an undertow.
Black frogmen leap
from yellow
lily-pad rafts,
a helicopter darts
and hovers,
like a giant dragonfly
dancing over the marsh.

Men with long poles
stir the shallows,
churn the mud,
cast hooked lines,
grapple the depths.
Bodies are pulled
from the water.

A mother and child
bundled, bagged,
and put on ice.
Carted away
in an ambulance.

Swift currents carry
us away, to home,
to work, to play.
The river flows on.
There is an undertow.
Do not go beyond this point!

Inside the Shadow

Autumn Twilight

A pair of geese glide silently
on the water, as the moon
and stars shimmer on
the ripples of Mill River.

Cool, crisp air carries
the fragrance of pine needles
and the scent of smoke
from a distant fire.

The old willow stands on
the river bank naked,
stripped of its leaves,
a skeleton of bark
and branches, scarred
and gnarled, a ghostly
apparition shuddering
and bending in the wind.

Still it endures,
rooted to the ground.

And at thirty-nine
I'm turning gray,
standing alone
on the river's edge,
wrapped in the mist,
wafting through
the cattail reeds,
watching summer's
dead leaves drift away.

To Walt Whitman

Your Long Island has changed.

The rolling Manhasset Hills running
along the North Shore are now rivaled
in height by landfill mounds rising out
of the South Shore marshes, their summits
obscured by sea gull clouds.

Gone are the potato farms, the land
has been divided and subdivided
becoming tract homes, Levittowns,
co-ops and condos.

Your leaves of grass are kept
green by chemicals, bordered
by fences, trimmed prim
and cut to village code.

Public parks preserve and protect
nature with chain-link fences
(so the trees can't escape).

Meadows are country clubs, the woods
are golf courses and pasture land
developed into shopping malls.
(In Huntington one bears your name.)

The pine barrens burned brightly
this summer.

Beaches are smaller, the sand
has been eroded or carted away,
but they are still accessible
(for a price; residents pay less).

Waterways overflow with pleasure
boats, are sometimes colored green
with oily rainbow slicks and aluminum cans.

You can almost walk across
the water now, but, then again,
you always could.

Cow paths are now parkways,
people are now cattle herded
into railroad cars bound for the city.

(I wish I had a prod to use when I commute.)

Traffic that leisurely flowed
across the East River
by the Brooklyn Ferry is now jammed
and clogged on bridges and tunnels
while, at night, electric street lamps
light the roadways out shining the stars.

Walt, let's face it, Long Island
is caught in the tentacles
of the Megalopolis, it has been
fileted, the head chopped off
and swallowed by the city.

The middle is life-less, over-
indulged, bloated, and the tail
wags as a playground for the rich,
the Paumanok is a dead fish.

An American Story

A short, choppy,
Post-Modern comment,
buckshot spewed words,
shedding bitter tears.

Chaotic, unstructured,
and totally meaningless.
It whispers a woeful lament,
live hard—die fast.

The character, an anti-hero,
feels like discarded garbage,
and is consumed by the calculated
ambiguities and ritualistic
suicide committed in America.

Experience transient paranoia,
milk crates for chairs,
and a large wooden cable spool,
(courtesy of LILCO), as a table.

An outlaw past, filled
with motorcycles, fights,
drug dealing, and gun running.

It's a rock and roll ride with psychedelics.

Watch the strobe
and black lights flash,
burn and tarnish
as bubbles float
drip, drop, lava lamp,
amid drift and decadence,

personality disorders,
narcissism, cynicism,
hedonism, nihilism,
a witch's brew
of antisocial behavior.

A classic example of bad taste,
morbidity, plot-less naturalism,
a misrepresentation of American
history, society, philosophy,
and psychology.

Soon to be a major motion picture
appearing in a neighborhood near you.

The Gate

I grew up in a cul-de-sac
off of Main Street,
nice houses, paved walks,
backyards, trees and shrubs,
it was all so middle class
with picket fences around
the lawns of manicured grass.

A rustic bulwark of tightly
piled rocks and stones, held
in place by weight and gravity
shielded the entrance on both
sides of the street from the sights
and sounds of passing traffic.

I was forbidden as a child to go
beyond this point alone.

I would go up to the corner at night
to watch and listen, cars and trucks
coming and going, flashing lights,
the buzz of electricity, cacophony
and symphony of movement, the beat of life.

And I would dream of wandering
down that busy road, flowing
in two directions and visit
the intersections of side streets
that could lead to anywhere.

By the time I was a teenager, I saw
the wall as an ornamental facade.

Catholic School Dance

In 8th grade,
Sister Regina proclaimed:
"*Mad Magazine* is communist propaganda;
reading it could damn your soul!"
She also said:
"All babies that die unbaptized go to limbo;
they have the stain of original sin
on their souls. But all aborted babies
are innocent martyrs and go directly to heaven."

I asked if we would be better off
if we all had been aborted.

I failed religion that year.
Sister Regina told my parents
I was reading 'Mad' magazine.

Later, in high school,

Brother Larry joked,
"The church only recognizes limbo
as a dance, everyone is innocent
until they reach knowledge
and awareness of their actions."

But who sets the bar?
Are we still unaware
or are we all stuck
in limbo, doing a dance,
seeing just how low we can go?

The Intersection of Broadway and Franklin

Afternoon showers cooled the August twilight.

I sat on the corner sipping a coke,
        smoking a cigarette, and eyeing
the girls outside the yahoo saloon
      across the street.

Cars rolled past, the tires hissed
       and spit on wet pavement.
You could feel a vibration in the air,
      the sound of heavy metal
thunder in a canyon.

Pedestrians stopped and stared
      at the horde of bikes rolling
        up to the light.

The girls oohed and aahed.

Harley choppers, hard-tails
    with extended front ends,
        stretched out to grab the road.
The motors growled with idle power.

The riders were hard core,
    statuesque, imposing figures,
dressed in tee shirts, dungarees,
    engineer boots, and black
leather vests, flying club colors
    on outlaw rockers.

The lead sat stone faced,
    a grizzly bear in sunglasses,
rebellious, independent,
        something wicked,
            something American.

Dark and dirty,
    clean and chromed,
pan and shovel heads,
    waited to dig the road.

At the green light,
    throttles opened,
        clutches popped,
            engines roared,
                fury released.

The girls mobbed the curb to watch them ride away.

They raced down the road,
    rumbling and howling,
        the echoes waned and faded,
            the passing of a summer storm.

At fourteen I knew what I was going to be.

At The Strip Mall

They meet at night,
a hodgepodge
of young punks,
greasers and hipsters;
adolescents
racing to shed
their virginity,
hanging out
under the neon
lights on hot
summer nights.

Fast food,
rock and roll,
hot rods,
and loud bikes,
image
and emotion,
id and ego,
the tug of war
to belong
and
to break away,
a noxious alchemy
of teenage
counter-culture
fusion.

Wary of the blue
knights
of the Galahad
squad,
they chill out
in back, up

by the railroad
tracks,
light up and blow
a joint,
smoke shaggy dog
hashish,
swill cold beer,
pop a pill,
and chase it
down
with Wild Turkey.

Feisty wards
of the American Dream,
under
the exotic narcotic
extortion
of youth, killing time
between
twilight and dawn,
childhood
and adulthood,
suffering
from the unbearable heat
of being cool.

Tanked

There is an ambiance to the Inn.

The rustic décor and a line
        of motorcycles
                parked curbside.

The old man sips his scotch
        at the end of the bar.
Sawdust spread over
        the splintered floor,
covers plywood patches,
        soaks up spilt booze.

Loud music blares,
        rhythm out of sync
                with the beat.

Cool breezes blow
        through the door,
college boys in country club dress,
        take a walk
                to the other side.

Smoked glass mirror
        distorts reflection,
cigarette smog hangs,
        halo lights glow.
Green algae tints
        the aquarium glass,
piranha drift in water,
        bikers swim in beer.

Goldfish splash
     in the fish bowl,
preppies slosh
     around the bar.

Feeding time,   happy hour.

Bubbles float,
     drip, drop,
         lava lamp.
    A push,   a shove,   a punch.
Strobe and black-light flash.

   A frenzy,   a fury,   a fight.
Big fish eat little fish,
     ashes burn and tarnish.

Jukebox rust drips in the air,
     blood stains
         the sawdust floor.

The catfish stick to the bottom;
the old man sits in the corner
     drunk.

Scooter Tramps

Every night hard core
bikers and 'wanna be'
warriors hold court
in the back of the bar.

They run their mouths
like they rev their bikes
as they rule the pool table.

It's all talk; about bikes,
pickup trucks, easy girls
and new tattoos, while
they guzzle down beer
with shots of booze, and share
their adventures of parties,
bike runs and brawls.

      Past,

          present,

             and future.

And they're all in uniform dress:
      black leather jackets
          or cut-off denim vests,
with stylish accessories;
      primary chains,
          hunting knives,
             and leather wallets
          chained
             to their belts.

They live for their big V-Twin
      Harley Davidsons,
and believe in an American Dream,
      the freedom of the road,
          the freedom to be wild,
and the freedom to be left
      alone.

It's an easy rider existence
      shackled to a lifestyle.

Ladies in Waiting

Outside the bar
sixteen and seventeen
year old princesses
dress in tank tops,
tie-dyed tee shirts,
cut denim shorts,
and Indian skirts,
smoking cigarettes
and drinking
from wine sacks
and bottles of Jack.

They moon-dance under
the neon lights
and dream of bankers
and brokers
driving white
Corvettes
to carry them away,
but tonight they settle
for black leather
bikers on Harleys.

They are the wild flowers
that fills empty spaces.

Let the Hammer Fly

Ride down
Ocean Parkway
on a summer night,
suspended
above the ground
on a thin
metal frame,
flying on
two wheels,

accelerating

until the trees
and shrubs
along the roadside
blur,
and the broken
white lines
blend
into
one.

You are Thor
riding a cloud,
thunder rolls
in your wake.

The Thing

Did you see it?
Did you hear it?
Did you feel it?
Did you smell it?

Or at least taste it?

Do you get it?
Do you know what I mean?
Do you know what I'm talking about?
Do you have any idea?

I didn't think so.

Frost Bitten Hands

The old English Professor
stood up from the barstool.

"An old goat they call me!
       Nay, I say.
I'm just an old poet,
       who's pissed—
off with their heads I say
       to the purveyors
of this new style of poetry."

He pounded the bar with his
fist and broke the glass.

"No form, reformed, conform, deformed,
       free-form performance
has turned the oral tradition
       into a blow-job, it sucks
the life out of the language, words
       don't convey image
they are all scene but not heard
       of cattle grazing at the coffee shops
and bookstores—Fifties style,
    It's all pretty beat to me."

His hand was cut and dripping blood.

"But enough of this crap;
       get me another drink,
two fingers of scotch straight up, no ice.
       And don't give me any of your bull-
shit, son!"

We wrapped a towel around his hand.
This was the price for being a mason.

The Lament

The guy in the green fatigue
jacket nodded out at the bar,
beer bottles and shot glasses
followed him on his way
to the floor.

The bouncer and the bar tender
helped him to his feet.

"No more for you tonight, hero."

He stumbled in a stupor
to the door mumbling,

"I'm no hero because
    I didn't stay in school.
I'm no hero because
    I didn't run to Canada.
I'm no hero because
    I wasn't captured.
I'm no hero because
    women and children were killed.
I'm no hero because
    I did what I was ordered to do.
I'm no hero because
    I didn't die over there.
I'm no hero because
    we lost the stupid war."
The door closed behind him,
and everyone just looked
    the other way.

Sales Pitch

Mad Mike was a businessman
with the devil's grin.

"Have I got something for you."
He pulled out a chrome silver
pistol, a talisman, gleaming
under the streetlight.

"It's a compact twenty-five
caliber, semi-automatic beauty.
You can hide it anywhere."

He slipped it into his pants.

"Look, no bulge."

He placed it in my hand
and I played with it,
sticking it into my
pants and jacket pockets
and in my belt front
and back, practicing
a quick draw.

"You can pull it out as easy
as flipping the finger
and squeezing the trigger
lets the sucker know
you mean it."

It was enticing and seductive,
beautiful and dangerous.

"It's for only a hundred
and twenty-five dollars."

I handed the gun back to him.

"How can you say no to owning
the pocket-sized power of God."

Last Night

At four A.M.,
Johnny was unconscious
on the couch, under
a cloud of smoke.

The eight ball of crack
was gone, the last rock,
melted away.

Carol Anne ran from window
to window, ranting about
the 'narcs' in the trees
coming to bust in the doors.

Mike was on the floor,
doing the carpet crawl,
prospecting the rug
for wayward rocks.

And I was shaving the mirror
with a razor for remnants.

I looked myself in the eye
and scraped up a piece of sanity.

It was time to leave
this nightlife behind.

Terminal Velocity

He raced past in
the opposite lane.

On-coming headlights
chased him off the road.

He hit the pole dead on.

The bike laid twisted
like a pretzel,
the rear wheel turning,
engine running,
racing to nowhere.

He was sprawled
on his back,
helmet cracked,
face mask smashed,
his eyes unfocused,
darted back and forth.

Red froth gurgled
from his mouth,
his body shuddered
and then stopped.

"Dave! David!"

He didn't answer.

The bike roared on.

His face was frozen,
contorted.

Shock,
     fear,
        confusion
              or awe?
I wasn't sure.
I looked into his eyes
and only saw myself.

There was no answer.
The motorcycle whined out,
sputtered and finally died.

i

I look in the mirror,
a two-dimensional image,
tired, worn, unshaven,
a touch of gray, aged,
skin and bone,
memories, scars,
feelings, tattoos

face to face,
blood shot and aqua-blue,
infinite reflections
within the eye
on the I,
study the pupil,
the darkness,
my being,
no past, no future,
only now

essence decoded,
the physical
and spiritual,
chronicled
and catalogued,

my life reduced:
a biological function
a chemical reaction
a mathematical equation

I cease to exist,
I become
the square root
of negative one.

Suspended Sentence

Is this where you held court?

Out in the woods,
in the clearing
surrounded by nature,
the judge's chamber
and jury box, above,
in the trees.

You were sentenced
to life without parole,

no mercy,
        no appeal,
                no lo contendre.

Condemned to dangle
        between
heaven and earth,
by the string of lies
        tangled
with knots of truth.

Was there any reasonable doubt?

Beneath the bow of the tree
the rope lays strewn on the ground,
uncoiled like the carcass
of the serpent cast out of the garden.

Are you free now?

Hey Bobby,

Hey Bobby, you're overdressed.
Suit, tie, jacket,
and a carnation;
I almost didn't recognize you
without your leather.

Do you feel out of place?

I see you're packed
and ready to go;
leather jacket, ratty
cut-off, and your cap,
all folded neatly
on the side.
Beer, Jack Daniel's,
and cigarettes
right next to you.

Pictures of your wife,
your kids, and your bike,
all the things
you liked, loved,
and lived for crammed
inside a box.

Are you going to miss them?

Hey, Bobby,
it's a going away party.
The guys are giving
you a toast, wishing
you a safe ride. . .
while the girls sit crying
with your family.

They miss you already;
but you remain silent.
I thought you liked parties.

How does it feel to be
the guest of honor?

Well, I've got to say good bye now,
I wish you could stay longer.
It won't be the same without you;
but you chose to live hard
and die fast.
I'll miss you Bobby B.

Do you think there are bikes
wherever you're going?

Daedelus' Step-Daughter

Angela climbed to the roof
of the apartments and spread
her wings to fly away.

She longed to be a butterfly
gliding across a wild flower
meadow, free on the breeze
of a sunny day.

But she fluttered
    like a moth,
        back and forth,
            boys, alcohol,
                and drugs.
So she leapt for sky,
    but the bushes
        broke her fall.

"Why?"
*"Because it was raining and I wanted
to see the sun."*

Nursed back to health,
in a fog of 'happy pills,'
she said she saw the light.

She finished the vial
and smiled,
"I don't need these any more,"
and found
      a taller
         building.

Mike and Mark

Two friends
too drunk
to drive
too cool
not to.

Drove
too fast,
took a turn
too sharp,
too bad.

They were
too young
to die.

You Are Gone

The experience ends,
    memories linger.

Tide and time,
    ebb and flow,
crashing waves
    spray the haze
of remembrance,
    revealing only

bits,
    pieces,
        fragments,

washed up driftwood
    and
broken shells,
    scattered
on weathered
        rocks.

Endless Wake

Death was not unexpected,
and after years of
lingering, no one took
notice of the passing.

The funeral procession,
plain and simple,
a red wheelbarrow
instead of a hearse,
mourners let out a howl
and said Kaddish
at the unmarked grave,
behind the decaying
stone wall in the wasteland.

A memorial is held
inside the Emperor's
Ice Cream Parlor and Café.
Street corner gurus
and kitchy schooled
coffee house bards,
spout and spew words
filled with cramp antonyms,
a grumpy con,
a gospel of prose,
a song of praise sung
with allegro hoopla.

Poetry is dead!
Long live poetry!

Grave Sight

From Mount Hebron
Cemetery,
stones and
monuments
roll
with the hills
into
the horizon,
until
they blend
with the city
skyline.

The buildings
look
like towering
tombstones,
giant
mausoleums,
new pyramids
for the new
pharaohs.

Outside the Garden

Stationary

I stand on the platform
waiting for the train,
while the bells toll
from the cathedral tower,
a cloud of pigeons
begins to flap and flutter,
shaken from their nests
in the eaves and arches.

While the bells toll
from the cathedral tower,
the faithful congregate
and flock to Sunday mass,
shaken from their nests
in the eaves and arches,
it's a reflexive response,
a ritual of existence.

The faithful congregate
and flock to Sunday mass,
while from Monday to Friday
they trudge into work,
it's a reflexive response,
a ritual of existence,
an attempt to navigate
the Skinner's Box of mass transit.

While from Monday to Friday
they trudge into work,
they are herded like cattle,
crowded on to the train,
an attempt to navigate
the Skinner's Box of mass transit,
and the 7:09 west bound
local arrives and then departs.

They are herded like cattle,
crowded on to the train,
a cloud of pigeons begins
to flap and flutter,
and the 7:09 west bound
local arrives and then departs,
I stand on the platform
waiting for the train.

Post Modern
(A cross words puzzle.)

The American poet   a pest muralist
     of words   paints
         with noun and verb.
Oily androids
     wait
     for the exiled orator
from the cul-de-sac off
         of Main Street.
Where noble angels,
         slicker eagles,
     and other con artists
ascend on high.
While,   the villain Caesar
       lies
asleep on mattress
       of canoe pie crust,
     custard weeds
surrounded   by platoons
     of rose sergeants
         in garden recitals
     of Athenian quartets.

Greek laurels,   Roman sobs,
      a melodrama
of cynicism and hedonism.

      Another nihilistic   (ersatz)
imitation shoves   out of line
      a spectrum
       of genuine peers
escorted to entitlement.

A long journey,   a backward task
      of torrid entrapment
beneath the shadow
       of the black mountain.
In the wind flaps
     Ezra Pound on trial
a dormant doormat.

To Allen Ginsberg

"Aware Aware where ever you are, No Fear"

On Saturday afternoon
I was stopped at a red light,
fishing for a cigarette,
listening to tunes,
when the radio broke the news,
you were gone.

They called you a "pop icon,"
"The Counter-Culture Guru."
But for me you are
an American poet and teacher.

Your howling long breath verse
gave inspiration and taught me
not to straddle the white picket
fences that separate and delineate,
or to worry about what fertilizer
my neighbor used on his lawn,
it's all cow manure anyway.

You forced me to look in the mirror,
beyond the two dimensional image
of America and focus on the background,
as you gave a voice to the disillusioned
and words for their disenchantment.

They called your work radical
and abstract, obscene for its time,
like Whitman, you told it the way
you saw it and passed that vision on.

And I am sorry that I never met
you in person.
This is my loss, and I will miss you.
I'll always have your words.
I will not say Kaddish, only
Thanks,
    Peace,
            Good bye. . .

Over Exposure
(a dialogue)

"What will you do if you get the grant?"

"I'll go to the slums of Calcutta for a photo shoot."

"India? Why there?"

"I want to capture the effects of poverty and starvation."

"Can't you do that here in an inner city ghetto?"
"No! I need a third world setting. I want to show
the squalor, suffering, pestilence, and death."

"They're building nuclear weapons, now. Do you think
your snap shots will change the situation?"

"I don't know; maybe the images will draw attention
to it."

"Oh, like on a TV documentary. I still don't think
everyone gets the Big Picture."

"Well, neither do I."
"What do you mean?"

"I only have a 19-inch set. I don't think I could handle a life-
size Doogie Howzer."

Cameos
(Another Inn Crowd)

I have to wade through
the crowd to get to the bar.

Ralph, the artist, sashays
from table to table, wanting,
waiting to get noticed.

He used to be into bikes,
but now he's into style.

He wears a bird's talon
earring to go with his
peroxide dyed crewcut,
trimmed with strokes
of pink and purple,
flowing into a six inch
black rat tail.

He's Ziggy Stardust
meets the Wild One.

Clad in a black leather
jacket over a red
and white striped
tee shirt, cut midriff,
finished off with blue
spandex pants
and snake skin boots.

Ralph wants to cruise
the Village clubs
for the "new sound"
he calls "punk."

The guys say he's gay,
but only *his* hair dresser
knows for sure.

Smoke wafts through
the air, a mixed fragrance
of incense, pot, and tobacco.

I breathe deep.

And Charlie "Cool"
is on the scene.

He comes in early on
weekend nights
to catch a buzz;
he's only here for the cheap
beer and booze.

Later, he'll go club hopping.
Tonight he's going disco,
slicked back hair,
wide collared silk shirt,
open,
so the braided gold chains
dangle
from neck to hairy chest.

He bops across the old
wood floor looking for
"girlie biscuits,"
his version of a love potion.

For Charley,
love is a combination
of physical attraction
and chemical reaction,
QUAALUDES solve
half the problem.

"Eight-ball in the corner,."
rises above the din.

That's JR, or Johnny Reb,
another biker, another fixture
by the pool table, always
with his gray suede Confederate
cap and a cigarette sticking
out of his mouth.

"Rack'em up!"
You can always hear him
before you see him.

I jump into a gap
at the end of the bar
and sit on the stool
next to Levy, "The Music Man,"
who is tapping the bar
and banging every glass
and bottle he can reach
with his drum sticks,
keeping the beat
to the jukebox music.

He can play the piano,
guitar, sax and drums,
and he jams with the bar
bands on the weekends.

He dreams of making it big,
but he has to get out
of this little place.

And after two shots
of Turkey and a beer,
I can blend in
like a chameleon
and party with them all.

But as the night wears on,
discussing girls and bikes,
art and music, slipping
into philosophy
and deteriorating
into a ranting monologue
of politics and religion;

I never wonder
whether my mug
is half empty or half full.

Outside the Garden

All around the city you see them,
they push shopping carts filled
with their sole possessions,
and pick up bottles and cans
for nickels.

They nap on park benches
in the summer or over
heating vents in winter.

They panhandle on street
corners and subway platforms
or inside Penn Station
and The Port Authority.

They feed at dumpsters
and seek refuge in basements
of burnt out tenements,
or use makeshift shelters
of abandoned vehicles,
the stripped shells, carcasses
of Lincolns and Caddies,
that seat six, sleeps three.

We try to ignore them,
and view them as nuisances
and pests, when we encounter
them on the street.

But from the penthouses
between Park Avenue and Columbus,
we all look like ants.

46

Salon

How do you like it?

Long and flowing,
luscious and layered,
curled, maybe?
Colored? Highlighted?
Slicked back?
    Or
do you want
      to just let
         it hang?

Be mysterious.
Let style set form.
Let form set the mood.
Make a statement.

Short and choppy,
cropped, spiked
or shaved to
the bare skin.

Less is more.

Oh, it's so retro!

You know, minimalism,
"It's the 'Thing'."

Poetry is like a haircut.

The old man dressed
in a wrinkled gray pin-
striped suit and ripped
canvas sneakers, sleeps
on a crushed cardboard box
outside the vestibule of the church
at Fifth and Fifty-First.

He has a sign above a shoebox.

Please Help Me
I have No Job and No Home
I Used to be Somebody

Patchwork
(Aids Day)

In the park,
a quilt of cloth,
        a blanket of clouds
a memorial,
        a darkness,
love and memories,
        ominous and foreboding,
color and design,
        shade and shadow,
covers the meadow,
        shrouds the heart.

And the list goes on:
        Alex, Michael,
           Kevin, John . . .
        names sewn together.

a lover, a brother,
        a son, and a friend . . .
        people sewn together.

And as the light breaks
through, there is a sunset,
painted in pastels,
        untitled,
           unsigned,
        in silence,
           a good bye.

Picnic

On Saturday, I watched
him hobble down
the path right through
the crowd gathered
in the park.

On-lookers gave wide
berth and stared from
a distance.

He reminded me
of Jesus on his way
to crucifixion.

Barefoot and shirtless,
unkempt brown hair
hung down
to his shoulders,
and a wide-eyed, blank
stare on his scraggly
bearded face, stared
into the infinite.

One hand grasped the untied
lace belt of his loose
fitting pajama bottoms,
and an old soda bottle filled
with water was under his arm.

In the other hand
he held
a gutted pigeon.

He found a bench
to lounge on as he was
having squab for dinner.

Medusa's Overbite

I looked past the ripples
in the reflecting pool.

Her image replaced mine.
The face of a chiseled
goddess, framed
with fiery red hair,
curled like a coital
knot of snakes.

Her dark eyes burned
         with desire.

I was seduced.

But her ruby lips
parted, revealing
a gap between her
yellowed buck teeth,
a darkness,
         a blackness,
         an abyss.

Reality is only the consensus
of similar perceptions.

Central Park Ramble

I entered the park at 72nd Street,
where "Imagine" is written in stone,
and wandered down the drive, across
the old bridge, over the mist
that veiled the other shore.

I followed the blacktop path
to the fork in the road
marked by a gnarled oak tree
clinging to life, its roots twisted
around a slab of granite.

Going to my left,
I saw the gray walls of the castle
on the hill rise above the trees,
access to it was cut off,
isolated by a cross-traffic
canyon, you can't get there from here.

At the comfort station
a guy in drag and a cowboy
pose outside the men's room.

"Gotta extra smoke?"
"Yeah." I obliged.
"Need a boyfriend?"
"No thanks."

They were just waiting for somebody,
anybody, to cruise on by.

I wandered past the out-cropping
of bedrock to the clearing,
a patch-work of shade, shadow,
and sun, spread over the carpet lawn.

Couples on blankets, picnicking,
snuggling, men and women, men
and men, women and women, someone
for everyone to move on and out
of the darkness into the light.

I strolled by the boathouse,
across the drive, said good bye
to Alice, Hans, and Humpty,
watched the sailboats slide
and glide over the reflecting
pool, and I faded on to Fifth Avenue
held down only by the pull of gravity.

A Four-Story Drop

Fresh paint
spilt on
the portfolio.

Red and black
paw-prints
dance across
the carpet.

Curtains blow
from an open
window.

Sandra weeps,
a suffering
artist, sobbing,

"The cat, the cat
is gone!"

It wasn't curiosity.

Suicide Spiral

James has no job,
    no place to live,
        only one place to go.
            To the corner,
                to look for crack
            the crystal death,
        the seductive
    kiss of death,
and then back
    to the basement,
        down in the dark,
            flick the Bic,
                light the fuse,
            bubbling,
        crackling,
    from solid,
to liquid,
    to vapor,
        one deep breath,
            no more problems,
                all gone
        in a puff of smoke,
        blackout
    the peace of death,
this piece of death,
    one bag at a time,
        one drag at a time,
            never enough,
                never forever,
            he always wakes up,
    he always needs
more.

1. *Choreography*

On the corner of Post
and Seymour,
dealers and buyers
perform
a business dance.

Wide eyed junkies
and wired crackheads
do the zombie shuffle.

Coke whores
and party girls
wait to cut in
and do their hustle.

Big and bold,
'POST POSSE RULES,'
is scrawled
on the building's walls.

A gentle reminder
of who calls the tune
on this street.

2. Little lambs

A flock of children
parade
through the playground
on their way
home
from school.
Mothers and grandmothers,
the wary shepherds,
guide
them through the maze
of beer bottles,
cigarette butts
and plastic vials,
that litter
the sidewalk
and fill
the empty cracks
where weeds
and grass
don't grow.
The women
try to keep
the children
in line,
and can
only pray
that as
their young
get older
they won't
stray.

3. Play Ground

On the basketball court
young boys talk
about taking the good shot
or making a slam-dunk.
Outside the fence
teenage boys,
too cool
for games,
and too old
for pop guns
and pea shooters,
kill time,
get high
on beer and wine,
listen
to hip-hop
on a boom box,
and talk
of Mac-10s,
Tech-9s, 8-Balls
and Uzies.
Out on the street,
it's about money
and power
where manhood
is measured

by caliber
and millimeter.

4. One Exit

Dried blood
stains, framed
in a chalk
silhouette,
a Rorschach
test
beneath
bullet holes
that climb
the wall like
Jacob's ladder.

Small circles
and tiny
flags
mark spent
shell casings
scattered
like seeds
on the pavement.

The yellow
police tape
defines
the border
in the blind
alley.

5. Reflections in a Puddle

After the hard rain
water run-off
from the street
fills a depression,
the pothole
on the side
of Gun Hill Road.

Children float
wooden sticks
as boats
and toss in pieces
of brick,
imagining the ripples
are waves crashing
on a beach.

Rainbows appear
whenever gas and oil
mixes with water.

6. Outskirts

Below the street,
the subway station
echoes
with the haunting
wails of
a saxophone playing
"Amazing Grace."

A girl shuffles
up and down
the platform,
shaking a cup,
asking for change.

Gaunt
with hallowed
eyes,
a veneer
of skin
covers a skeleton.

She says she has AIDS,
she begs to live.

A poster on the wall reads:
"Take the train to the plane."
It's an escape
to the suburbs,
to anywhere,
out of sight,
out of mind.

61

Heat Wave

Looking for relief,
I sat on the fire
escape sweating out
the eighty five plus
degrees of the muggy
July night.

I watched the gibbous
moon rise, it hung
above the horizon,
a big, juicy slice
of orange over
the skyline.

I wanted to reach out,
bite into it and quench
my thirst.

At Saint Agnes Cathedral

I look up toward the spire
where the crucifix is crossed
with an X like an asterisk *.
I wonder if there is a footnote?

No Change at Jamaica

"Tickets please! All tickets!"
click-click, "Thank you."

The train rolls out of the tunnel
into the twilight,
   the Hillside railyard,
   Swingline Staples,
   DKNY,
10,000 Sq. Ft. for Lease or Rent,
   Please Call—Realty,
through Woodside,
   Forest Hills,
   Kew Gardens,
over Queens Blvd. and the LIE,
   cars, cars, and cars . . .
past factories and apartments,
  buildings and junkyards.

"Jamaica, Jamaica, this is Jamaica Station."
"This is a Freeport train stopping at
Rockville Centre, Baldwin and Freeport.
Change here for all other stops."

 "All aboard."

Pass on by Sutphin Boulevard,
   York College,
   NY Telephone,
cars and houses,
  stores and parks,

passing through St. Albans
　　　and Rosedale,
spires and steeples,
　　　churches and synagogues.

"Tickets please! All tickets!"
click-click, "Thank you."

Running parallel to Sunrise Highway,
　　　The Sunrise Multiplex,
　　　Green Acres Mall,
schools, offices,
　　　gas stations,
and restaurants.

Racing into Valley Stream
　　　and out of Lynbrook,
grass and trees,
　　　ponds and streams.

"Rockville Centre, this
is Rockville Centre."

The train slows, enters
the station, and I'm down
on the street, standing
outside the cathedral
once again.

"Tickets please! All tickets!"
click-click, "Thank you."

Train of Thought

When I boarded the express,
Lao Tsu punched my ticket.
Jesus, Krishna, and Buddha,
were sitting, playing cards.

"Poker?" I asked.
Lao Tsu said,
"No! It is the game
that cannot be named,
it is the eternal game."

"What?"

"The nameless is the beginning
of heaven and earth."

"God," Jesus chimed in,
"We're playing God."

"And who is God?" I asked.

"I Am," the three replied in unison.

Moses and Mohammed were watching.
"And what about you?" I asked.

"We don't gamble," they answered.

They were only conductors,
so I asked, "Who is the engineer?
Who is driving this train?"

"You are," was their reply.
"Where am I going?"

"The tracks are laid,
follow the signals."

I got off the train.
I'm in no hurry
so I think I'll walk.

Facing the Wall

Modern Americana

This is the land of freedom of choice:

Coke or Pepsi, light beer or dark,
less filling, tastes great,
Republican or Democrat,
horse manure, cow manure,
different crap, same smell.

America is now a pie divided
into eight slices,
but there are twelve at the table,
and three of them want seconds.

It's all a game.
George and Martha never had a son.
Truth and illusion;
it doesn't make a difference,
we still sit in the waiting
room expecting delivery.

Money is the new Messiah,
greed is the national creed,
"In G-O-D (gold or dollars) we trust,"
but credit cards accepted.

The government of the people
has been bought and sold.
It's only business, nothing personal.

The heart of America stopped
beating, the blood clotted,
no longer red, now mediocre,
and pumped by the pacemaker
of public opinion.

The real American patriots
are true blue and white
or least act white, and all
the stars are in Hollywood.

U. S. A. *

Accounts payable
Mortgage due
Economic hardship
Revenue sharing
Inflation
Cash flow problems
Audits
Nausea

Depreciation
Real estate
Exorbitant spending
Allocations
Myth
*(usual state of affairs)

Facing the Wall

58,202 names
    engraved on a black reflective surface
58,202 names
    JOHN H ANDERSON JR. on the west end
58,202 names
    slowly piling up to the middle
58,202 names
    1959 to 1975
58,202 names
    DALE R BUIS meets RICHARD VANDE GEER
    at a 121 degree angle of eternity
58,202 names
    the Alpha and the Omega
58,202 names
    receding back down
58,202 names
    JESSIE C ALBA on the east end
58,202 names
    "Who took the time to count them all?"
58,202 names
    "Daddy, this is a sad wall."

A Passing Fear

```
                    Frani
                 climbs out
               of the shower,
             wrapped in a pink
           bath towel, pats herself
         dry, ties     back her hair,
        wipes the      mist from the
        mirror, and    stares at the
        naked image.   Her face has
       good color.     Smooth.   Youthful.
       Her body is     trim, firm, and
      shapely. She     raises her right
      arm and with      her left hand
      performs the      periodic ritual.
       Her fingers      probe her breast
      and underarm,     gently squeezing,
       searching for    lumps, bulges,
         tenderness or pain. She finds
        nothing and repeats the process
          on her left side. She'll be
            forty in a few months and
            have a mammogram, another
             procedure she'll have to
            endure every year, because
            she's at risk. Her mother
            lost her right   breast
            over twenty    years ago,
            she's alive,     but, Gram'ma
            died from the    cancer, long
            before Frani     had been born.
            'And what if     I have it,
            lumpectomy,      mastectomy,
            or should I      take the test
           to find out if    I have the gene,
          and then what if   I do? Have both
          removed and         reconstructed,
         still losing a       piece of myself?'
       " Mommy, why are        you crying?"
       Frani's five            year old asks,
       from the threshold      of the doorway.
       "It's nothing,          honey, I have
       something in            my eye."   She
       rubs her eyes            and wonders
       'Will my daughter        have to face
        this, or will            they ever
         find a                  cure?'
```

Dusk

Without
direct
sunlight
to cast
shadows,
the form
and
essence
of an
object
become
one.

For W. C. Williams
Easy Zen

Oak tree
simple
roots,
trunk,
bark,
branches,
leaves,
buds,
acorns,

complex
birds,
bees,
squirrels,
spring,
summer,
autumn,
winter,
life,

simple,
oak tree.

Bethel, NY
8/15/98

I sought higher ground
and settled next to the totem
of Jerry, Jimi, and Janis
on a crest of the hillside.

Above me was the tented
Rock and Roll strip mall,
everything from
tee shirts and crystals,
to computerized stereo sound
systems and cell phones.

There were convenient ATMs
and credit cards accepted.
Buy a piece of flower power,
but don't sell your soul.

The Woodstock Nation had come of age,
an attempt to balance its moral ideology
with science and technology
and blend it with the realities
of commercialism and materialism.

And below the music played on
to the crowd that danced and swayed.

Melanie, Donavan, Richie,
Lou, Joni, and Pete,
sang of peace and love,
human rights and wrongs,
life in the gritty city,
spirituality and ecology.

Once again,
Sisyphus struggles to push
a boulder of manure up hill,
knowing it will roll
back down to the valley below,
and he smiles with hope
that from the seeds
of art and music, something
good will grow.

To Galway Kinnell

Dear Mr. Kinnell,

With the deepest sorrow I inform you
of the passing of Betsy the Bomb.

Her last spark plugs fired
not long after the day we
journeyed from SUNY Farmingdale
to the train station in Wantagh.
You kept her spirits up
by not complaining about
the dirty windows, rusty
exterior, ripped car seats,
and dusty interior.
And after the long bumping,
rattling ride, in my book
you signed
'For Peter and "the Bomb."'
She was so thrilled she made
it home with barely a misfire.
You'll be happy to know that
Betsy's battery, stereo,
and speakers have been trans-
planted into another vehicle.

In lieu of oil, please pay
for the tow.

Verse

Paper
blank,
mind
blank.
Oh,
blankety-
blank!

Writer's
block.

Mother Nature

she turned toward me,
her eyes took in
the infinite,
"I speak down to you,
because you are beneath me . . ."
sex is her weapon,
she wields it well.

A Brief History of Valentines Day
and The Big Bang

I was pulled
into her black-hole
by the irresistible
force of sexual
attraction.

Sucked into
the vortex
of the void,
I penetrated
the event horizon
and time ceased
to exist.

Stretched and elongated
I exploded and collapsed
into the singularity
of our being.

We created three universes
that night.
Later we had wine, smoked
cigarettes, and laughed.

Genesis Reprise

We danced naked
in the darkness.
The universe revolved
around us, a vortex
on the grassy field.

Wet grass reached
up like fingers,
grasped our feet,
clutched our legs,
and dragged us down.

We rolled and writhed,
groped and stroked,
a glowing energy,
a cool incandescence,
we melted,
into each other,
into the earth.

We were the stars, shining
brightest before the dawn.

Crap-Shoot

Venus and Mars
Tom and Viv
man and woman
Ted and Sylvia

make love—wage war

rolling together
a pair of dice
alone

we die

drifting apart

a pair of ducks
on the river
of life

black and white

ripples

circles around

yin and yang
you and I
XX and XY

is the only
real question.

Love Letter

To Lisa:

My love for you is like the ocean.
Well navigated on the surface,
but mysterious
in its uncharted depths.

Unchanging in flow, but flowing
with change like the force
of a hurricane that batters the coast,
its power washes away
all that stands in its way and then
returns to placid serenity.

Sometimes my love may seem to recede
or ebb only to rush back,
like the rising tide reclaiming its domain,
cleansing away all our yesterdays,
renewing our beach with the currents
of fresh, new feelings.

And as the sea is eternal, existing
prior to all life, bringing forth all life,
and continuing long after
all life has perished;
so is my love for you,
always constant, and as everlasting
as the ocean.

Kevin's Calling

He recites his mantra,
"He dribbles, he shoots, he scores."
Basketball is his religion,
and he worships the Chicago Bulls.

His bedroom, a shrine filled
with posters, knick-knacks,
a throw rug of a basketball court,
a locker, and a hoop with a backboard
that stands in the corner.

He has two changes of sheets,
blankets, and pillow cases
for his bed, and the dresser draws
are stuffed with tee shirts,
shorts, sweat pants and jackets,
all in the red, black, and white
motif of the Chicago Bull's Team colors.

A picture of the Trinity:
Jordan, Pippen, and Rodman,
hangs over his bed.

After high school he plans
to attend the seminary
at the University of North
Carolina, do missionary work
with the USA Dream Team
and, later, be ordained
into the priesthood of the NBA
at the cathedral of the Chicago
United Center as a member
of the Bull's order.

I guess at four years old
you have to believe in something.

Wisdom

I watch him in the shopping center spinning
like a cyclone, as the breeze twirls paper
and leaves in the corner of the stores.
He says,
"I'm doing the wind dance."

And on a summer night, under the streetlight,
He pirouettes with his silhouette partner, saying,
"It's time to do the nine o'clock shadow dance."
So when I was rushed to do some errand
that seemed important at the time;
he called to me,
"Hey Daddy! Look, there's a butterfly!"

"Hurry up, Kevin, we've got to go." I answered,
"I've seen thousands of butterflies."
"But, Daddy, this is just one butterfly."
You can't argue with a four year old.

Ritual

12:01 A.M.

In the dark
I hear the faucet,
drip, drop,
keeping time
like a clock.

All that I've done,
all that I am,
never happened,
never was.

It's an instinctual
performance
like a rat
in a Skinners' box.

-check the stove,
-lock the door,
-turn off the TV,
-look in on Kevin,

and in the glow
of the night light,
he whispers,
"I love you Daddy."

I am back again
and, as I go to my bed,
I wonder,
Did I set the coffee maker?

April Boardwalk

The shops are all
closed,
'REMODELING'
for the coming
season.

Sporadic joggers
clop
      on by
and the occasional
bicyclist
      rolls
          past.

The sky is overcast
and the wind
        chill
makes fifty degrees
feel like
      thirty.

The beach is desolate,
cleared
      of the ocean's
winter
      refuse.

The sand is virgin
of foot prints,
      marked
      only by endless
lines of wind
    sculptured ripples,
      running
perpendicular
to the waters
      edge.

The waves don't break,
they roll
      gently
and kiss
      the shore.

Seagulls hover
      and land
only on
      the jetty rocks.

And I sit
   on the bench,
sipping coffee,
      thinking
about the poem
I haven't written,
          yet.

The Jetty

I climb the stone slabs
haphazardly placed,
extending from shore,
an unfinished bridge
to nowhere.

The black-gray rocks
break
the rhythm of the waves
and send salt spray
into the air.

With the delicate steps
of an acrobat,
I cross
the slippery crags
to sit on the jagged edge,
look out on the ocean's
horizon to span serenity.

Post Script

Do not try and read
between the lines.

_____

_____

_____

They have been left
blank for you to fill in.